Journaling
Through A
Breakup

How to Effectively Cope Through a Breakup Without Gaining 50 lbs. or Becoming Anorexic

N. Newman

For information contact :
nancenewman.com

Book Cover design by Pixel Studios

Editing by HappySelfPublishing.com

DEDICATION

To my mother and my dear friends who survived
my breakup with me.

Acknowledgements

First and foremost, I want to thank my mother for her unconditional love and support, for being my sounding board and always listening without judgment. Everyone should have a mother like you.

Thank-you De and Marsha for being the dearest and truest friends anyone can ask for. Your love and encouragement has held me up many times. Thank-you for your advice, for brainstorming with me, and for all your great suggestions and contributions to my book. I couldn't have done it without you!

Genine. You are one of my truest friends, definitely my biggest fan and my grammar police. I am forever grateful.

Table of Contents

Introduction…....………..…………………….………1

Step 1: The Breakup 9

My Journal: My Breakup 21

Step 2: Journaling to Get Through the Day...................26

My Journal: How to Get Through the Day....................38

Step 3: Journaling to Explore Your Emotions...............41

My Journal: Explore My Emotions 58

My Journal: Have Some Fun-Fantasize 74

Step 5: Kiss Off Letter..77

My Journal: My Kiss Off Letter....................................85

Step 6: Substitution 88

My Journal: What Are My Substitutions?.....................96

Step 7: Self-Discovery and Revelation 105

Step 8: Owning Your Life Through Owning Your Journal 127

My Journal: I Own My Life 133

You Made It! 142

About the Author………......……………….……....…144

Extra JournalingPages……………………………...146

Introduction

In today's world, breakups are an everyday normal occurrence but when it happens to us, there's nothing normal about it. What we don't realize is that breakups last much longer than the initial announcement that your spouse/partner wants out. Breakups continue long after from the verbal split, to the physical split and even beyond.

There is so much to deal with; your feelings, separating possessions and maybe moving, the pets, friends and family and possibly children. It is so overwhelming you wonder how you will get through without gaining fifty pounds (if eating is your comfort) or becoming anorexic (if stress keeps you from eating)—neither of which is any good for our bodies.

You start to ask yourself how you'll be able to get through this. Will you be able to manage and/or control the range and intensity of the emotions that you keep feeling? You want to get your power back, take charge of your life and you want to feel good again—to feel happy and not have to worry about where you're going to live or who gets the dog.

How do you navigate down the toll road of a breakup? I say it's a toll road because it feels like you have to pay your way through the whole breakup process whether it be material (you lose your house, half your possessions), physical (you cope by eating and gain too much or the stress keeps you from eating and you lose way too much weight) or emotional (you lose control over your emotions because they are overpowering and in a constant state of flux).

This book tells you my story and how I used journaling to sanely get through the most difficult phase of my life—how through journaling I caught myself heading down the dark road towards being anorexic and was able to turn myself around. I'm happier than I've ever been and I didn't think I could be.

I'm going to show you how my journaling process can help you to get through a breakup (especially a nasty one) and come out the other side in a better, solid place. I will guide you through the journaling phases that will enable you to navigate down your own breakup toll road so you can find your way through the maze of emotions and take control of the glitches, snags and complications that you will face in order to become a happier and healthier you.

My eight step journaling process can not only help you through a breakup, but it can also help you to overcome any adverse event in your life, whether it's being laid off from your job, the death of a loved one or even an illness that is mentally and emotionally holding you back.

You'll learn how to deal with your emotions, gain control of your feelings and pacify your anger. Through journaling, you'll learn how to finally let go and say good-bye not only to your relationship and your spouse but also to your negative emotions when you write your own Kiss Off Letter. You'll also find ways to combat the resulting loneliness and finally to self-evaluate so you can learn from your mistakes. In the end you will find your independence, your power and your happiness.

I've been there. I know what it feels like to see the world as you knew it come to an end. I know what it's like to feel the overwhelming sadness and anger consume your every waking minute. It can prevent you from really living. It can be the blanket that covers you on the couch as you lay there not wanting to work or be a part of any social life.

I read lots of books on how to let go of your relationship as well as some on how to deal with your sadness. They didn't help me. I went to a therapist, but for me, it wasn't enough. I began journaling the day I found out my spouse was breaking up with me and I realized it was the only time I felt in control. Because I was being reluctantly pulled into the world of breakups, I needed to make sense of what was happening to me, why it was happening and how to deal with it. Journaling provided me with a way to do this.

Journaling is known in the medical and psychological fields for the positive benefits it presents to the patients including reducing stress, solving problems, and resolving disagreements. We face all of this and more during the collapse of a relationship. The stress is sometimes unmanageable because there are many issues to address and problems to solve and most times they can produce some very nasty disagreements. Journaling will help you to find peace of mind in war like situations. It can help you to be a better person, one who can keep a level head during the breakup process.

I promise that if you follow my journaling method, you will find ways to manage yourself and your world around you during a difficult time in your life. You'll be able to make sense of what you're feeling and why you're feeling it. It will help you to sensibly make decisions that you need to make without giving up more than you should.

Most importantly, you will be able to find the strength and courage to take a look at your relationship and recognize what was wrong so you can take ownership for the part that you played in the breakdown and realize the mistakes you don't want to repeat.

I promise you will find a road to take to a better you, a stronger you, a happier you. I believe what

6

made this process successful for me was that I was my own therapist. I had to do the work if I wanted to get off that couch and enter the living again. You can too!

Don't wait to start journaling. Don't let someone else rule your emotions and your actions. Don't let the destruction of a relationship destroy you. The best thing you can do for yourself is to rise above it and not only show your ex that you are in a better place, but feel it as well and you can do this by journaling your way through your breakup.

Journaling will help you to crawl out of that hole that was dug for you and then you were pushed into (even if it's only inching your way out). Then you will bury the remains of your broken relationship in that same pit and stand triumphantly on top.

People will be impressed and say," I don't believe how well you are handling it," and you *will* be able to handle it well if you read my story and start journaling your way to a calmer, happier and stronger place in your life.

At the end of each chapter and at the end of the

book are pages for you to start your journaling to a better, stronger you.

Step 1: The Breakup

The first step is to acknowledge there is a problem. Whether you lost your job, was diagnosed with an illness, lost a loved one or you are going through a breakup, you have to acknowledge that something is wrong and you are about to go on a journey you didn't expect to go on and don't want to take. It will be hard, but you can do it.

For the purpose of this book, I am going to talk about the end of a relationship—a breakup.

Someone told me a long time ago, "Once a cheater, always a cheater." I'm the type of person who wants to believe the best in people. A cheater can change. Well, in my case I was proven wrong. I still hope that cheaters can change, but mine didn't.

The funny thing was I went back. Again. And again. And again. And once more. What does that make me? "Once a wuss, always a wuss?" See? That's why I like to believe that people can change, because I sure wanted to after my final breakup.

Let's be honest. Breakups suck. Plain and simple. It doesn't matter if your husband, wife, partner, lover, whoever cheated on you, moved to another place on earth, couldn't commit, wasn't *in* love with you (one of my favorites), doesn't like your family, liked you when you first met but after getting to know you—not interested. I could go on and on with the reasons, but there is only one thing they all have in common. Breakups are like bailing out a boat that has a one foot hole in the bottom using a small Tupperware bowl. When they first happen, it feels overwhelmingly hopeless.

What's worse is when you are on the receiving end of a breakup; you usually don't have a choice. It is handed to you. Like a summons. Here you go. I'm officially breaking up with you on this day of this year. Thank-you very much. I especially like the breakups done through text (courtesy of the new technological age). A phone message is bad enough, but a text? There are all sorts of ways to break up with someone, but they all share the same, sad truth. You're left on a deserted island with a message in a bottle that says it's over. In the end, you're still alone and you've got nowhere to go.

Now there are those people who are going to say breakups aren't always bad and these could be the small percentage of people who split amicably or those that are delivering the bad news. I know there are plenty of good reasons out there to break up with someone, but there are a lot of bad ones too. However, you need to remember that the person delivering the bad news wants to end the relationship because they already know the direction they want to take in their life. Still, delivering the breakup summons to someone can be devastating as well.

Ending a relationship actually takes a long time even though it may seem as if it happened to you in a day. It might have started before when you were experiencing deep down subconscious suspicions— the ones that you don't admit even to yourself but they are lurking around in your psyche. Or you noticed you and your spouse were having slow building disagreements that festered into constant squabbles and then full blown arguments. When the breakup happens, you hit yourself in the head and ask "why didn't I see it?" But you really did.

If you're fighting, you try to find reasons to stay away to avoid the constant confrontations. You feel your spouse isn't listening to you. You can't reason with them and they're not compromising. They are emotionally moving farther and farther away from you and you don't know how to bring them back.

If you're suspicious, you try to peer over their shoulder to see who texted them or who called - not admitting to yourself or to anyone else what you are doing. But you can't get to their phone because they keep it attached to them like a diabetic who wears an insulin pump. It is their life line and if it gets taken away, all hell could break loose.

You show up at places you know they frequent. They tell you they're going to the gym. You tell them to have a good work-out and suddenly, you feel the need to work out yourself even though you haven't wanted to in weeks. You start suspecting everyone who is around them might be the one who is taking their attention and time away from you—the fitness coach at the gym, co-workers, neighbors, the cashier at your local grocery store.

It kind of makes you sound like a lunatic doesn't it? Well, that's what unsolicited breakups can do to you which brings me to the next point. When you don't want a breakup, you try to be who you think they want you to be as your last ditch attempt to make them want to stay. You go back to where you were and who you think you were when you first got together.

Wait a minute.

Isn't that who you are now and who you've been all along? Well, yes and no. Let's face it. Most relationships change over time because we too, change over time. But our fundamental selves remain the same.

The first weeks or months of a relationship are exciting-full of kissing, cuddling, sex, and feeling exhilaration from your head to your toes. Everything old seems new again because you are experiencing your life as you've known it with someone new—looking at it from a different perspective. So you want to go back to that—find that spark that you think you've lost.

But all that has happened is that you've settled in to the comfort and love of the relationship, so it seems things…change. You learn more about each other and some of those things might not be to your liking. But you love that person and isn't that what love is all about? Acceptance, giving, compromise, and most important—unconditional love?

At this point, all some people can hear is blah, blah, blah. They can't handle it when relationships get to this stage so when it all falls apart, they think if they get back to the beginning, their spouse won't want to leave. But you see, even though you may be able to go back, you won't be able to stay there because it's not who you are anymore and most times by now, your spouse is already emotionally gone. I think we all know that when our spouse is emotionally gone, they're gone and nothing can bring them back.

So here is the next point. DON'T. GO. BACK. You'll find I mention this a few more times throughout the book.

I speak from experience. Most of the time, going back doesn't work. Besides, in the end you will see that you deserve better than that. Someone just slammed the door in your face. Why would you want to open it back up? So they can slam it in your face again?

It's all about the control and if they are the one who slammed the door, they are in control. The funny thing is, you can be the strongest, most independent person in the world and someone can still take your power. There are all types of people who are good at this and when you lose that sense of direction, independence and control, it's tough to get it back.

The breakup process is actually now just beginning.

One of you might have to move. Maybe there's a house to sell, children to think about and who gets the dog or the cat? There are possessions to split and friends that will have to take sides because it's almost impossible for your friends to play Switzerland. Ultimately, they will have to choose a side.

A breakup is hard enough but now you have to cope with all of that while your heart is breaking and when your heart is breaking, to say there is a plethora of feelings is putting it mildly. These emotions could include:

1. Disbelief-How could they do this to me? Why did they do this to me? What did I do wrong? Maybe I should have done things differently.

2. Anger-How dare they do this to me? How dare they cheat on me and embarrass me? Often, the anger builds and gets out of control because you're forced to make decisions you never thought you'd have to.

3. Sadness-My life as I know it is over. I don't want to get out of bed. I don't want to go to work. I think about it all the time. I cry all the time. It's a loss and we all know loss is the biggest sadness of all.

4. Confusion-You were just blindsided. What the hell just happened?

5. Failure-I never thought I would be divorced or separated. I don't know what I did wrong. What's wrong with me? Another relationship gone bad. Why did I fail?

6. Uncertainty of what's next-Do I buy another house? Rent? I have to think about and consider the kids and/or the animals. Where do I go? What am I going to do? Do I need to find a job? Do I need a lawyer? Why do I need a lawyer? Do I have to change my address and maybe my name on EVERYTHING?

7. Revenge-What can I do to get them back? This one is definitely not good but let's face it, most of us have thought about it or dreamed about it.

8. Regret-I wasted all my time. If I hadn't gone back I would be well on my way in life and probably happy with someone else.

9. Grieving-They haven't died, they just left you. Sometimes it's harder to know that

they're still alive because that leaves a little crack in your thoughts where you might believe there is still a chance that you could do something to win them back. If they had died, that possibility would not be there. They're gone. Period. Nothing you can do will bring them back so there is no crack that hope can creep into.

10. Fear, panic-One day my life is in total order-I know how it is going to be. Now it's all gone. What do I do? Where will I go? How will I be able to afford to live, to pay my bills? I'm all alone. Will I be able to get a job? Who will be there for me?

You are now on the biggest, crappiest emotional roller coaster of your life that you've ever been on and you're not sure the seat restraint is going to hold. And for the next "however long it takes to finally be done with it" (if you can be done with it), you will run the gamut of the above emotions almost every day.

You want to sit on the couch watching soap operas and eat the five gallons of ice cream you bought right after you received your breakup news. You've had thoughts of taking the Brooklyn Bridge even though you live in Los Angeles or maybe you contemplate spending all your money to go see the Dalai Lama to find the meaning of life.

But none of those will help.

So, how do you work through all these emotions while you're breaking up, deciding who gets what, possibly dealing with lawyers, all the while trying to keep yourself sane and your children (if you have any) protected from everything you're feeling and going through? How do you turn and walk away from that door and stay away so you can take your control back?

How do you deal with it all - how do you become whole again?

You journal.

Really.

You're not getting out of this that easy. So, let's get started today because you have to get through today.

Turn the page and start your journal. Get a pen and write down how your spouse broke up with you and why they did (if you know why). I've put a few sentences down for you to help you get started. Don't be afraid of what you're thinking or feeling. It's time to start so you can begin to take control of your feelings and your life.

One thing you should remember is that this is not the time to worry about grammar, sentence structure or content. This is all about you and what you're feeling no matter how it comes out. It might be a bestselling thriller one day, but you'll have time for re-writes later.

My Journal: My Breakup

Name_____

Date_____

How did your breakup happen?

_____

_____

_____

_____

_____

_____

_____

_____

_____

_____

_____

_____

_____

_____

_____

_____

_____

How did you feel when they told you?

_____

_____

_____

_____

_____

_____

_____

_____

_____

_____

_____

_____

_____

_____

_____

_____

_____

_____

_____

What things will you need to work through after the breakup (move, divide possessions, pets, friends, children, family)?

_____

_____

_____

_____

_____

_____

_____

_____

_____

_____

_____

_____

_____

_____

_____

_____

_____

_____

_____

How does it make you feel?

_____

_____

Step 2: Journaling to Get Through the Day

Journaling is not your Facebook page. This is not a time for you to have hundreds of people telling you what you should be doing or knowing all about your business. This is the time for you to figure it out on your own and frankly, I just can't read one more breakup story on Facebook. And if you're having a mini breakup-skip Twitter too!

In this section, we're going to talk about the second step of the process—how to get through the first days after you find out your relationship is unraveling. It will be a time of total unrest in your head and your heart. Your mind will be spinning so fast it won't be able to stop on any one sane thought.

Now is the time you might want to eat yourself to

oblivion or starve yourself because the thought of food is revolting. You have to get to a point where you can start thinking sensibly because there will be important decisions to make and you have to make sure you take care of yourself so that they are made with a sound mind.

Many of us don't have the money to see a therapist and most people can only afford to go once a week for an hour. What do you do the rest of the time? How do you get through the next 167 hours until your next appointment? You have to get to the root of the problem soon before you fall apart. How will you be able to make important decisions when you find it so difficult to function?

You need to figure out what went wrong because something did go wrong somewhere and whether you like it or not, you had a hand in it. It might be as simple as you didn't heed all the warning signs so you kept going back, or as difficult as accepting your role in the breakdown of the relationship before the summons appeared.

You may not be able to afford a therapist, but you can afford a piece of paper and a pen, or like so many today, you have a computer or a smart phone.

There is no right way or wrong way to journal. It is yours and yours alone and once you start you will find it easy to continue, but as you're reading this you're probably wondering how to start, where to start. Exactly what is journaling and what will it do for me?

I will be honest and say when it comes to journaling for me, sometimes the handwritten word on a piece of paper is so much more powerful, but if that isn't for you, there are many journaling programs you can put on your computer or your phone (just Google journaling programs) or you can record your thoughts and feelings on a recorder. The key words here are record, log, chronicle, document, write down.

Whether you write with pen and paper, type using a keyboard or talk into a recorder, the important thing is to get it out of your mind and somewhere where you can sort it all out. You want to look at it from an unbiased viewpoint so you can make level headed decisions and begin to heal your heart and your mind to become whole again-to be the person you always were and most importantly, the owner of your power.

When my spouse handed me the breakup summons, my world stopped. Literally stopped. I couldn't eat, sleep or function at my job. I lost thirty pounds in under a month and the people in my family who weren't aware of what I was going through thought I was terminally ill. I was forced to move on top of it all and I didn't know where I would go. To add insult to injury, I found signs of cheating—pictures, notes, and was subject to continual lies and transgressions.

I was almost three thousand miles away on the other coast for work when I received the call that we just weren't working anymore. My spouse wanted out. I begged and pleaded to wait until I got home so we could talk about it. My spouse said there was nothing to say. What made the most difficult situation of my life even harder was that for the next five days, there was nothing I could do - not three thousand miles away. And when I got back, we were closing on a house and moving the following week.

I panicked, I felt sick and for those next five days, confusion and disbelief took over my mind. I needed to talk to my spouse but they didn't answer the phone. Now you could throw anger into the mix.

The overwhelming feeling of possible loss and being lost was what drove me to take out a piece of paper. There was no one to talk to. My friends and family were three thousand miles away and even if they were in the same city as me, I wasn't ready to tell them my marriage was over because I convinced myself it wasn't. See the confusion?

I started to write down what I was feeling and what I hoped would happen when I got home at the end of the week. I'm sure you know that what I hoped was going to happen, wasn't going to happen. My spouse wasn't going to open their arms to me and say "I'm so sorry, I had a lapse of a sane mind" and then hand me a bouquet of red roses (this is where you roll your eyes).

Writing it down helped me to function for the rest of my work week. Anxiety still ruled my body, but writing down my feelings, my hopes and dreams helped me to get through an almost impossible situation. Even though my hopes and dreams were not going to come true, it didn't matter. The only way I could hold on to my sanity at that point was to hold on to my hopes and dreams. Later on, though, I would need to make new ones and journaling helped me in that process as well. We will visit this in Step 7.

As you probably guessed, there were no open arms or roses when I walked off the plane. My spouse was there in body, but that was it. The ride home was silent and as soon as they dropped me off at home from the airport, they left. At that time, I thought it was just too painful for my spouse to be around me because I kept trying to talk about their decision.

I didn't even unpack my suitcase. Instead, I opened my briefcase and took out the sheets of paper that had my thoughts and emotions scribbled down on them. I reread what I wrote and once more confusion and questions ran through my head

It went on like this for a week. My spouse totally avoided me until we had to meet at the lawyer's office to close on our house. We tried to get out of it, but it was too late. What made matters worse was we had all our friends and family lined up to help us move. I knew I wasn't going to tell them because I still had those hopes and dreams that things would just iron themselves out.

Fear that this wouldn't happen was thrown in with sadness and anger that was building over the days. I needed to keep control of my emotions so I could function, so I continued to write down the events as they happened. I wrote about what I was feeling, followed by the options I thought I had, which seemed very limited.

Journaling kept me sane but that didn't mean I did the sanest things. Everyone will do things differently and that is my point here. You have to do what is right for you but in the beginning of a breakup, you really don't know what that is and you shouldn't make rash decisions. Journaling helped me sort out what was happening and how I was feeling at that time. Writing down the few options I had kept me from making decisions that I might regret later.

I wasn't ready to let go even though if all my

friends and family knew what was happening they'd probably scream at me to get out. So did journaling help me make the right decision? Maybe not in their eyes, but it was the right one for me at the time.

At the end of the week, we painfully moved. Together, and even though I didn't tell anyone what was happening, they all knew, especially when my stuff went in one room and my spouse's stuff went into another. How can you keep up a real smile, honest laughter, and ecstatic small talk as you move into your new home with your partner all the while omitting the fact that they probably won't be your spouse for very long and you could very well be homeless?

I'm sure you're getting the picture by now.

It was hard to talk to a person who left every chance they got, which continued after we moved and THAT should have been an important sign. Where was my spouse going? Why didn't they stay so we could work this out? These were the questions that ran through my head every day. So during those times when I was staring at the walls and the countless unpacked boxes because I had no idea what was occurring around me, I pulled out my journal and addressed these questions. Suspicions jumped out at me from the pages.

Once again, I wrote down the events of the day, how I was feeling, questions that plagued me and as the days lumbered by, I began to acknowledge the signs of cheating. Floodgates opened. I cried all the time. To stop the crying, I pulled out my journal and began to write about my anger because my anger was building. My partner not only wasn't giving us a chance to make things right, but I was beginning to realize that it might never be right because they were already emotionally gone. I tossed and turned between sadness, fear and anger. Mad one minute, scared and afraid of the unknown the next.

Writing down these emotions helped me to keep them under control. I still had to go to work and I wasn't ready to tell my co-workers either. But I'm sure the fact that I was still hurting, I was still sad and angry and afraid of the future gave it away. So I wrote in my journal, a lot and when I wrote about my feelings or wrote down something that happened during the day, I felt the anxiety leave my body enough to give me the strength to take another step and face head on what the next day brought.

When I got home from work, most times my spouse wasn't there. Nothing had changed in the house since we moved in. Boxes were still unopened; only the essentials were unpacked. I pulled out my journal and wrote down how lost that made me feel. Through my writing, I realized I didn't want to feel lost, so I started to sort through the boxes splitting our possessions. Somewhere in my thought process, I knew it had to be done and this gave me the capability to have a little control in a situation I thought I had none. Besides, my spouse was never there so why would they care?

These feelings can be so overwhelming, you may find nothing helps. Sadness can lead to depression if it's not dealt with. There is also appropriate anger and inappropriate anger that can lead to bad things—like revenge. If journaling isn't helping you to move forward through these feelings, you may need to find the money to see a therapist. Journaling may not work for everyone and you may find that you're stuck in the negative feelings and you can't seem to gain insight to your emotions so you can move past the breakup to a better place. An important thing in any breakup is realizing when you have to get outside help. Don't make a mistake and ignore this.

It is important that you are able to keep your feet planted on the ground while your emotions are flying all around you. Journaling about what's going on in your life will help you to do that. It will also help you to start the process of being able to sort out all the feelings that are flooding your psyche so you can take control when you both start to make important decisions. You need to have a voice in those decisions and not let your spouse walk all over you.

It's time to address what's happening to you each day. All it takes is to write one sentence, only one, even if it is as simple as "I am pissed" or "Today, my spouse was a jackass." The rest will pour out of you once you get started.

Remember—this is not the time to worry about grammar, sentence structure or content. This is all about you and what you're feeling no matter how it comes out and writing about your emotions might get you that bestselling thriller one day.

Turn the page and start to write about your day. Give details about what's happened during the day even if it's just that you sat in front of the television and cried all day. It will be important later on.

My Journal: How to Get Through the Day

Name_____

Date_____

Talk about what happened during the day. Did you go to work? Did you eat? Did you stray from your usual routine and if so, why?

_____

_____

_____

_____

_____

_____

_____

_____

_____

_____

_____

_____

_____

_____

Talk about your feelings during the day. What
feelings did you experience? Explain what
happened to make you feel that way.

_____

_____

_____

_____

_____

_____

_____

_____

_____

Step 3: Journaling to Explore Your Emotions

Don't kid yourself into thinking you don't have to do the work. This step is one of the most important steps of the process. It's where you dump out the puzzle pieces onto a table and start to put them together all the while working towards the assembling the whole picture.

Journaling to help you get through the day was just that—a way to help you get through the day so you could get to a point where you can begin to explore your emotions enabling you to get through the total process of the breakup and be in a decent state of mind to make good, sound decisions for yourself and be in a good place.

Journaling about your emotions gives yourself permission to feel whatever it is you're feeling whether it is disbelief, anger, sadness, confusion, failure, uncertainty, fear, revenge or regret. Even though all you may feel is anger, there is so much more beneath that anger.

The combination and order of your emotions won't make any sense because you could be feeling several of them all at once every day and they could be very different from day to day. Feelings are very personal and the things that evoke them are the experiences that you go through and these too are different for everybody.

There is no blueprint for dealing with breakup emotions.

Journaling at this point can help you to make your own blueprint. In other words, figure out what you are feeling, why you are feeling it and how to get to the other side without the negative emotions consuming you and making it difficult for you to function and/or make the important decisions that need to be made.

Through my journaling, I was beginning to see that the door mat to my life said "Wipe your feet here—over and over and over again."

When I realized my spouse was cheating on me, the breakup was in full bloom. The biggest surprise for me was the anger that was building and starting to consume me. The lies, omissions and betrayal started to take the form of a monster and there were times I wanted to snuff that monster out. Journaling helped me to write about it, but not do it. In Step 5 we'll talk about snuffing out the monster.

My writing became more frequent and much harder. Anger became the ink in my pen every day. It was difficult to get past the rage and be aware of the other emotions that were there. But as I wrote, my anger would decrease a little bit, allowing those other emotions to come to the surface. Being able to acknowledge those other feelings that were masked by my resentment and fury gave me some control over all my emotions. Now, I could take a deep breath, write about everything I was feeling and take the time to address and analyze each emotion I had. In doing so, I began to have a good hold on what I was feeling and why.

One day my spouse made the mistake of coming home when I was there and I took the opportunity to confront them. I was prepared as I remembered the words I put down on paper and the emotions that poured out. And even though at that moment, all I felt was anger, I was able to control it because I learned how to through my journaling. I recognized all my feelings, so the confrontation didn't come from anger alone.

I knew I didn't want to sound like a crazy, out of control person, but I *needed* to make my partner see how wrong everything they did was. I firmly believe if I hadn't been releasing all my emotions on the written page, my spouse might have seen a raving lunatic, or I would have crawled into the shadows and played the role of a submissive, injured partner letting my spouse get away with the crap they were pulling on me.

Instead, I was able to lay everything out on the table. The things I wrote in my journal were reaching out to me at that moment—the cruelty and cowardly way of breaking up with someone when they are so far away, avoiding their spouse because of their own guilt and the cheating ass my partner had become, leaving me hanging so I couldn't move forward. By the time I was done, my spouse sunk to the floor knowing they had been a total bastard and then some.

The more you write about an event including how you feel about it, the more clarity you will have. Writing about my experiences and feelings and going back and reading them helped me to see things I didn't see at first. One was the door mat I had become and didn't know it was a role I had been playing. The other was I knew I couldn't tell my spouse I hated them. I didn't. I realized I hated what they did and that was what I needed to tell my spouse. And that's exactly what I did. I told them how much I hated what they did to me, not that I hated them. Telling my spouse I hated them would only make the breakup process worse than it already was. And to be honest, there was still a part of me that wanted to forgive my partner and try to repair the relationship. I just didn't know if I could do that.

After my spouse left, I sat down and wrote about my triumph and the positive emotion I was feeling—a little bit of empowerment. I was able to communicate my feelings to my partner in a controlled way. I didn't say anything I regretted and that was a good thing for me. My journal writing helped me to sort out my emotions and make some sense of them.

Confrontation may not be the path you should take. You know your situation better than anyone. For me, it was a path I knew I needed to take and I was confident even though it was conflict, I would be safe. Always keep your safety in mind.

I knew I wasn't out of the woods yet, because my spouse still left me after the confrontation. Guilt didn't keep my partner from leaving, rather it made my spouse run even faster. So after I wrote about my small triumph and the little bit of control I had taken back, I wrote out different goals—more realistic ones. I had to do this because I was at a point where I was beginning to accept a little bit of reality. I didn't think my partner was coming back so I needed to look forward and decide where and what I wanted to do. When I came to this conclusion, I thought I was done dealing with my emotions, so I tried to figure out what to do with them. Park them in the garage?

The answer is absolutely not! If you put them away, they will actually lead you by the nose because they really aren't done (neither is the breakup). Not by a long shot. Parked emotions can make you say and do things you wouldn't in a normal and calm state of mind because you don't deal with your feelings when you ignore them. They start to fester underneath the surface and one day—BAM! You become that raving lunatic or do something you regret later. So, like it or not, you need to drive those emotions down the road with you for the whole trip.

Writing gives you permission to open the relief valve so your mind doesn't get overloaded. Putting your feelings down on paper (or in your journal on your electronic device) helps you to sort through all your emotions and try to process them without having to live them at every moment. And sometimes you can successfully let them jump off the written page like I did when I finally got the chance to confront my spouse.

You can deal with your anger easier by writing it down because taking all your emotions, especially anger, out on your spouse will most likely get you nowhere. My situation was a good example of this because other than the satisfaction I felt, my confrontation didn't get me anywhere—they still left. It could make things worse because your spouse might yell back at you or just close themselves off and not hear a word you are saying. This will only fuel your anger and it can lead to nastier arguments that can get out of control. You most likely will say things you wish you hadn't.

But…you can write those things down on paper that you want to say and know you shouldn't. I remember writing about the day I found some pictures of my spouse and their new love interest. I remember writing how angry I was, how much I hated both of them and how hurt I was that I wasn't good enough for my spouse, that they found someone better. I wrote down where and when I found the pictures and how stupid my partner was that they didn't hide them better. I also wrote that I wanted to dial my spouse's phone number and shout a few choice words that I won't write here but because I wrote the words in my journal, I didn't feel compelled to call.

I've already said it and I'm going to say it again.

Don't go back. Why do I say that? Because I did. In the first chapter, I told you I always believed that people could change. I still believe that, but writing about my story made me see something I didn't want to see. Not all people can change and it sure is hard to know whether someone is capable of changing or if they even want to change. It's also difficult to realize that you might believe a person can change because you don't want to accept that they can't.

We all need to have faith that people can change but believing because you want to go back to someone to end the pain and unhappiness that you are feeling, and because you think it will be easier than having to make all the changes and decisions that are facing you as a result of the breakup will only end up with that door slamming in your face once again.

Going back is not something you should do when your emotions are in a blender. Get them under control so you can look at your situation objectively and then make a decision that will benefit you and make you happy, not hurt you. If going back is the decision, then you have a better chance of making it work because you made that decision with a clear head and knowing what will be involved.

Looking at it now and reading my journals, I can definitely see that going back to my spouse was not necessarily a good thing. We had good times after I went back but things always fell apart and after the third time, I saw a pattern that neither of us was willing to recognize. We just kept playing it out.

I did go to a therapist at this point and against the therapist's advice, I still went back. The only thing that helped me to finally open my eyes and be able to walk away from the door that was once again slammed in my face was to re-read the mistakes I made over and over again. Someone once told me "if you always do what you always did, then you will always get what you always got." Obviously, going back got me the same thing—the slamming door.

Writing in my journal helped me to see things about myself that I was ignoring and I needed to pay attention to them. Remember the subtitle of the book? *How to Effectively Cope Through a Breakup Without Gaining 50lbs. or Becoming Anorexic.* As I mentioned earlier, I lost thirty pounds in under a month. My family didn't tell me until years later they thought I had cancer. For me, it wasn't eating too much to get through my emotional slump, it was not eating enough because food made me physically ill. I didn't see myself losing thirty pounds. I saw myself getting thinner and maybe more desirable. I looked in the mirror and saw I was losing the relationship weight I had put on over the years.

I bought new clothes to fit my new look. I was five feet seven and three quarter inches and was under one hundred and twenty pounds. My face was sunken in. I stopped looking in the mirror because when I did, I actually did notice it but I didn't want to see it. I ignored my weight loss as much as I ignored food.

The foolish notion in my head was that my spouse would come back to me when they saw how much thinner I had gotten. I told myself I gained too much weight during our time together and I needed to lose some, so I didn't see the red flag that I continued not to eat. In some ways, I probably had a little self-loathing going on. I had to come up with a reason as to why they chose someone over me. I wasn't good enough. What did their new love interest have that I didn't? What could I change to make my spouse want to come back to me? Oh, the sadness of it all!

I was a jogger. I ran five miles almost daily. Two weeks after we moved, I noticed I had to stop a few miles into my run. At the end of the third week, I was stopping more than once. I got mad. I needed to stay in good shape. My spouse wouldn't want me back if the muscles on my body got flabby (you can groan here).

I was perplexed and kept asking myself why was I having trouble running? By the end of the first month, I readjusted my running route because I couldn't run five miles. The most I could run was one to two miles. I sat down and wrote in my journal. I wrote how angry I was I couldn't run the distance I used to. I stopped to think why I wasn't able to do that and when I wrote that I felt weak and tired, my hand stopped writing.

I reread the previous week's entries since all this started. I had written down on different days how I didn't sleep at night and I wasn't hungry. I didn't always write what I ate that day, but looking at the words, I remembered that it wasn't much. Because of the events that were taking place in my life and the emotions that were taking precedence over everything else, I wasn't taking care of myself.

That day, I looked in the mirror—really looked at myself. It was a rude awakening. The image I saw staring back at me said it all and I didn't like what I saw. I was letting the situation and my emotions as a result of it take control not only of my psyche but my physical body as well.

I realized I didn't want one person to make me feel hurt, angry, scared, lost and inept anymore. I didn't want someone to push me so far into the negative feelings that I put my health at risk. And you don't either.

I had given away too much control over myself and my emotions. I started to write again but this time I made some goals that I would work hard to achieve. They included eating better, trying to get more sleep (maybe chamomile tea at night and watching comedies on television to give me good thoughts when I closed my eyes). I promised myself to take better care of myself.

That was a defining moment in the breakup process.

I decided the most important thing at that time was to concentrate on immediate, significant goals—the long term ones would come in time. This is what you need to do for yourself. Make the short goals, the ones that need to be made right now, taking care of yourself being the biggest one.

The last emotion that I want to talk about is loss and grieving. At some point you will realize that your ex is really gone, for good. For me, grieving came and went like a yo-yo. We were still living in the same house for a while before we started to make the decisions that needed to be made to physically end things. So when my spouse was home at the same time I was, I was thinking of ways to make them happy, keep them there, and do whatever my spouse wanted.

The pitiful thing for me was not only did my partner take every advantage of whatever I offered, but everything they did made me feel that they still wanted me, that they wanted to stay. It only made me hang on. So when my spouse left to go be with their other love interest, I was crushed once more and I grieved—again. Every time my spouse walked out the door I experienced everything associated with loss, even if it was for only one day or one night.

Every day my partner was with me, I wrote about how wonderful it was and how it would be great again but when they walked out the door and didn't come back at night, I cried. I opened my journal and wrote about how I had lost my spouse all over again, I needed to move on, and life was so empty without them. Can you believe what I put myself through? My relationship was like a tennis match and I am sure my friends and family who were on the sidelines watching were moving their heads back and forth as the plays went.

The point at which you realize the breakup is really going to happen and you're not going to be able to stop it is the time when you really start to grieve. You need to know that grieving will last for a while. You are experiencing a great loss and what makes it worse is that the person who walked out on you is still here on this earth, maybe around the corner, but you can't touch them. Sometimes this makes it so much harder to let go.

When a loved one dies, it is so painful, but

eventually there is the realization that they are gone from this life. You know you won't see them again on this earth or be able to touch them or talk to them (unless you believe differently). When we go through the loss of a loved one because of a breakup, there is the chance of running into them somewhere. There are many of you who still have to stay connected to your ex—maybe because of children, so even though you've lost them, they're not gone and that is not only painful, but it can make it harder for you to accept the loss because there's that very slim chance they might come back—that they *can* come back. You could find yourself in a stalemate.

Journaling about grief and all your other emotions will help you to eventually accept the breakup as a reality. You can put your emotions in to categories, and start to manage the feelings that want to take over you. Writing about them is a release—open the spigot and let them flow out onto the paper. It won't get rid of them right away, but it will lessen the intensity of your emotions.

With time, the what, when and why you are feeling will make sense to you. You will understand them enough that you might even be able to fight them off so you can perform at work, or make a solid decision that you know has to be made. When you get to this point, your anger might still be a big factor so in the next chapter we'll learn how to deal with the most volatile of all the emotions.

The real work starts here. Writing about your emotions can be tough. The best way to start is with one sentence as simple as "I feel sad."

For some of us, words may not be the way to go, so graphics are also encouraged. Take a piece of paper and doodle, or draw pictures that reflect how you're feeling or what is happening in your life at that moment. On the airplane home, I drew a stick figure holding a bouquet of roses. Several weeks later I went back and refined my drawing—the roses were wilted and the stick figure was hanging from the gallows. I will review this change in my drawing in Step 5.

My Journal: Explore My Emotions

Name_____

Date_____

Do you feel sad? Why?

_____

_____

_____

_____

_____

_____

_____

Do you feel angry? Why?

_____

_____

_____

_____

_____

_____

_____

Do you feel inadequate? Why?

_____

_____

_____

_____

_____

_____

_____

_____

_____

Are you afraid? Why?

_____

_____

_____

_____

_____

_____

_____

_____

_____

_____

Are you sleeping at night? If not, what is keeping you up?

_____

_____

_____

_____

_____

_____

_____

_____

_____

Do you find yourself not wanting to do anything but sleep or lay on the couch all day?

_____

_____

_____

_____

_____

_____

_____

_____

_____

Are you binging on food or are you not eating?

_____

_____

_____

_____

_____

_____

_____

_____

_____

How often are you crying? What makes you cry?

_____

_____

_____

_____

_____

_____

_____

_____

_____

_____

Are you accepting what's happened? If not, why
aren't you?

_____

_____

_____

_____

_____

_____

_____

_____

Are you feeling regrets? Why?

_____

_____

_____

_____

_____

_____

_____

_____

_____

_____

Are you confused, unsure of what to do next? Why?

_____

_____

_____

_____

_____

_____

_____

Do you feel like a failure? Why do you think you're a failure?

Do you want revenge? What do you think getting revenge will do for you? Is it worth the consequences?

Step 4: Have Some Fun-Fantasize Revenge

It's time to snuff out the monster.

In this step you're working towards releasing your anger. You might be angry at your spouse for dumping you, or a boss for firing you or laying you off. If someone has died, you could be angry that they left you, but revenge isn't a factor in this situation. So just write it down. Write why you are angry your loved one died. You could feel guilty about your anger. Using a journal will help you to realize that it's okay to be angry.

Now back to the breakup.

Let's face it. The moment you were handed your breakup subpoena, a little bit (or maybe a lot) of anger was lying deep beneath the surface of your other emotions. And if you are like me and found out your spouse was cheating, soon your anger will rule out all the other feelings.

We've all thought about revenge and sometimes we don't want to wait for karma to do its thing. But what you really don't want is for anger to take over and you find yourself saying and doing things that you will regret later. This alone makes you mad. You feel helpless. The son of a bitch will get away with ruining your life, hurting you deeply, turning your life completely upside down and backwards.

Because of this, anger can often get out of control.

So now, it's time to snuff out that monster that you once shared a life with (and I want to emphasize here that you will do this in theory only through your journal writing). This part of journaling helps you to soak in your fantasy revenge without actually doing it. Writing down how mad you are and how you'd like to deal with them helps you to experience these thoughts in the safe environment of the written page, or the typed screen.

Remember, your anger is for you and you alone. Writing it down helps you to put it away permanently so the last thing you want to do is to share it with social media. Again, it's not for Facebook, or Twitter or email. It's to be written in your journal to stay in your journal.

You are not only trying to heal your anger, you also need to protect yourself from it. So if you feel your anger is getting the best of you, try writing down everything that makes you angry and fantasize how you'd get even (or if it's really bad, get a therapist).

People write about this all the time. Many country songs have been written about getting revenge on a cheating spouse. Fiction books have been penned where the authors go into great detail inflicting their vengeance. Here's your chance to write your story.

One day I sat with friends and brainstormed revenge ideas. Some of their suggestions were to put sugar in the gas tank of my spouse's favorite car or throw a dozen eggs at the house I had to leave. Another was to setup a robo call that says "I hate you" repeatedly. And one of my favorites was to dump a load of gravel or manure in their driveway.

We laughed and laughed but that was what it was for—to release my anger through laughing. It was the next best thing to writing it down. So when I got home, I wrote all those suggestions in my journal. I even drew some pictures to go with them.

As it became a reality that my spouse was cheating, I not only had anger towards them, but I was seething at the other person who stole my partner and my life from me. I wanted them gone because foolishly, I thought if that person was gone, my spouse would come back to me—everything would go back to the way it was. It was all the other person's fault. They seduced my spouse with their sorceress ways. That person messed up my spouse's mind and held them captive (again, you can roll your eyes or laugh here).

Graphics at this stage were helpful for me. Remember the drawing of my spouse holding the bouquet of roses? Yes, you are right. This is the point when the roses got wilted and my partner was drawn hanging from a rope. Now I'm not an accomplished artist by any scope of the imagination. I draw stick figures. So I drew stick figures of them getting run over by cars, falling out of a boat without a life jacket and drowning, my spouse getting punched in the face, both of them falling off a cliff as they hiked—to name a few.

Sometimes I even made it like a story board and often it would make me laugh. I think it's here that authors can find some really good story lines. I also want to emphasize at this time that if you can make yourself laugh at this point, then you're doing well—your journaling is working.

Use your imagination. Have fun with it. Fantasize then put it away. Revisit it when you find your anger surfacing or your ex does something that really pisses you off like showing up somewhere that you are with "the other person". That actually happened to me. I went to a winter concert with a friend. We were sitting in one of the balcony sections and directly across from me was my spouse sitting with their new love interest. Needless to say I went home and drew stick figures of them falling out of the balcony and splattering all over the floor below.

Writing and drawing out my anger about the whole situation did a couple of things for me. The first thing it did was it helped me to keep my anger at bay. I was able to work through it as I wrote about it or drew pictures. By the time I was done writing and drawing about whatever made me mad, I was feeling my body relax. When I put my journal away, I put my anger away too.

After every entry into my journal (written or picture) that was about anger, I wrote the phrase "I will not let my anger get the best of me." Anger can be so blinding and there still was so much left to go through. I knew I wanted my wits about me when the decisions about the house, our possessions and the dogs had to be made.

The other thing this did for me was it made me realize that it wasn't really the other person's fault—not totally. They *were* a part of it and I couldn't ignore that, but I found myself not hating them. I really liked the other person, but I actually felt sorry for them because I knew eventually my spouse would do the same thing to them (and of course, it happened). It was then I had to admit that there are some people who can't or won't change

Keeping my anger at bay allowed me to forgive

(this is an important point here that I will visit in Step 7) my spouse and go back to try and make our relationship work. I'm going to say this again. Do. Not. Go. Back. It wasn't a good thing but when the next time rolled around, I came to a very essential insight. I realized that the first time my partner broke up with me I held my anger back too much. If I had kept a little of that anger on the burner, I might not have walked back into that slamming door.

Eventually, I didn't need to snuff out the monster anymore. By drawing pictures and writing about my anger, it started to dissipate as I became aware of these conclusions. It gave me an outlet for my anger so that I could examine it truthfully and in doing so, I began to let go of my anger, my relationship and finally, my spouse.

Now it was time to write my Kiss Off Letter.

My Journal: Have Some Fun-Fantasize

Name_____
Date_____

Draw a picture here of what you would like to do to your spouse.

Write down here all the things you would like to do. Make them as outrageous and fun as you can—not realistic.

_____

_____

_____

_____

_____

_____

_____

_____

_____

_____

_____

_____

_____

_____

_____

_____

_____

_____

Draw pictures of some of those things you listed above.

Step 5: Kiss Off Letter

This step is similar to a rite of passage. You've identified your feelings and worked through them to understand the what, and the why. Now it's time to let go of all your sad and/or negative emotions so you can move forward because often your feelings can keep you stale mated for a long time. If someone you love has died, it's not a Kiss Off letter, it's a Good-bye letter that might be filled with love. Writing a good-bye letter can be healing to you even though you may never be able to let go, but it will help you to move forward.

But if you were fired from a job or your spouse left you, then it's a Kiss Off letter.

So getting back to the breakup—you've journaled through the first horrible days and you were able to get past them. Then you journaled to understand your emotions, to make sure you let yourself feel them but not let them dictate what you're going to do. You've visited your anger through writing about it and maybe even drawing, and you've worked hard to understand all your emotions you've been experiencing since the breakup summons first appeared.

But there's one more thing you need to do. You need to let go. At this stage of the game, you're most likely going to have negative thoughts about yourself as well. You might be feeling inadequate, especially if you've been cheated on. So take a little time and go back and read your journal. Then take a page and put a line down the middle. On one side write down all the things that were good about your relationship. On the other side, put all the things that were bad, you didn't like or you didn't agree with.

One of the biggest things on the negative side will be the breakup. I believe that if your spouse/partner breaks up with you, then even though you may not think there was all that much wrong with your relationship, there was definitely something wrong for your spouse or with your spouse. The bigger point to see here is that either you weren't told there was something wrong, or you didn't listen. You should begin to see it now by re-reading your journal and having evaluating yourself, your feelings, your spouse and your relationship.

Now the big question becomes do you really need this relationship? Followed by the next very important question, do you really want this relationship?

If you answered no that you don't really need this, but yes that you want it, then you have a decision to make here. Do you go back? If you do go back, I encourage you to continue journaling, even on the good days because you might need it down the road. If you find yourself back here again, the journaling that you do during the time you are back together will be even more enlightening to you as it was for me.

I went back and my spouse did the same thing again. I looked at what I wrote while we were back together and what I found was I started to write about the good days but I didn't write every day because not every day was good. Soon, the pages transformed quickly to bad days and then I was writing every day because the bad days once again started to take over.

When I compared the journal I wrote during the second break-up to the one I wrote during the first break-up, it was a mirror image. I was able to take everything I wrote from both journals and make better decisions. What's that saying? "Fool me once, shame on you. Fool me twice, shame on me." So the next time I asked myself those two questions, the answer to both of them was no. It was time to write my Kiss Off Letter.

What is a Kiss Off Letter? It's the letter you write to someone who has disappointed you, hurt you, or treated you badly. You can't bring yourself to tell them face to face or maybe it's just not feasible (you have children and we all know the last thing you want them to see is you telling off their other parent).

It's the letter you write after you've done some work through journaling to tell that person exactly how you feel, what you think of their actions and that your life no longer revolves around them. You can survive without them. You don't need or want them.

It's a big step.

You don't need to send the Kiss Off Letter. Place it in your journal. The actual writing of the letter is all you need to do to end your dependence on your spouse. It is a rite of passage, so to speak, to move you to the next level of your breakup.

The Kiss Off Letter also helps you to begin setting up an expectation of how you're going to get through the first time you see your ex. Writing the letter will help you to feel what your brain is telling you—that it's over, really over and that you don't need or want them anymore, but it won't necessarily make you feel whole again.

Hopefully you won't run into your ex before this like I did. Remember in the previous chapter I saw my ex at a concert? The result was going home and drawing some interesting pictures and writing a few angry paragraphs in my journal. I hadn't gotten to the point where I could write a Kiss Off Letter, thus it was hard for me to see my spouse and their new love interest. I also eventually went back to my ex and had to go through this all over again.

I finally reached the stage where I wrote my Kiss Off Letter. At this point, I felt justified in writing it. My Kiss Off Letter was a good one and when I finished it, I felt separated from my spouse and from the relationship as if it never happened. I also felt a measure of satisfaction because I knew I was ready to move on—this time to really move forward.

My letter spoke about all the things my spouse did wrong in the breakup because it was the breakup that angered and hurt me, not the relationship. I wrote with strength of heart and conviction in my words. I told my partner how cruel and insensitive their actions were and if they had ever loved me, they would have respected me and talked to me instead of insulting me by calling me when I was three thousand miles away and telling me they wanted out because they couldn't do it anymore.

Months before, I was feeling inadequate, blaming myself for the breakup. I felt undesirable as the thought of all the things I could have done wrong when someone dumps us ran through my head.

Through my journaling, I came to acknowledge the fact that I too had a part in the breakdown of my relationship, but the actual breakup was indeed all my spouse's fault. And now, I had to voice that opinion and I did so in my letter. I needed to say that I was worthy of so much more and that my partner wasn't good enough for me and I truly meant that. It was an admission that I wasn't the door mat that I had been turned into. Instead of my door mat saying "Wipe your feet here, again and again and again," it now said "Just try walking on this, bitch!"

The Kiss Off Letter is a statement of letting go of all the negative feelings that have been plaguing you since your breakup started and in turn giving you the resolution to stand up for yourself. The letter can be liberating and therapeutic as you release yourself from everything that has been holding you back from starting the moving on process. The letter is final, but it's not the end. It signifies the beginning of a new phase of your breakup process, the one where you start finding your happiness once again.

In the next chapter, we'll begin the process for finding your happiness and your power that you thought you lost.

My Journal: My Kiss Off Letter

Name_____
Date_____

Dear………………,

I am done with you.

OR

Dear…………………,

Good-bye

_____

_____

_____

_____

Step 6: Substitution

No matter your situation, this step is the beginning of your healing and moving on. It can be a difficult step but if you tell yourself to look at the positive side of working through this step, it will be rewarding—the reward being your happiness.

You put the Good-bye Letter or the Kiss Off Letter in your journal, closed it and then stared at the wall. What's next? Even though you've taken your stand and you really are ready to move on, it's not over. You aren't finished because this is the time you will begin to feel a blank space in your life. But this is also the time when you begin to fill it and it can be exciting!

Feeling that blank space is normal. There *is* emptiness, a gap in your life because your relationship is over. Your spouse is gone. Maybe you moved so you no longer have the home you were comfortable in, the home where you put your heart and soul into. Now you're in a strange place. Maybe you lost the dog or cat to your spouse and for many, there is the split custody of the children.

There are holes in your life and you need to fill them. The next stage of journaling through a breakup starts now—substitutions for those voids you are feeling. It is time to start that new phase of finding your happiness.

Your goal here is to not remember your ex's birthday or special days—that they go by without upsetting you and eventually not even entering into your mind.

Now that you've gotten a hold on your feelings, you've dealt with your anger and have finally "kissed off" your ex, you're realizing the breakup process still isn't over. Here's that Energizer Bunny. It's still going, and going and going.

You come home from work and stand in the middle of the kitchen. You don't feel like cooking for just yourself. You haven't had the desire or the energy to make the new place feel like home because it isn't your home—not yet anyway. You don't feel like socializing. You don't have the company of the dog and your kids are staying with their other parent for the weekend. Now that the sadness, fear, confusion and anger are getting behind you and you've taken care of the decisions that you had to make, what's left?

Loneliness.

There's a part of you that wants to go back and I know this is a piece of what made me return to my spouse. I missed doing the things we used to do. I missed hiking with my ex, going out to dinner, watching a favorite television show while we cuddled on the couch, working outside in the yard together. Sure, I could watch television in my new, smaller house and work on the garden when the weather got better, but I didn't want to.

This is part of the grieving process. When you're alone and they're not there, you grieve but there is also a different kind of sadness. It was that sadness that made me pull out my journal. It was a little harder to get started this time because I thought I was on my way. I mean, I got through the worst of it—didn't I?

I found myself crying again so I wrote down the one sentence that summed up what I was feeling, "I miss my spouse." Then I crossed that out and wrote "I miss things from my previous life" because I didn't miss my spouse anymore. I missed the things we used to do, the possessions I lost in the split, and that's when the rest of my words flowed out onto the paper. I missed my house that I had so lovingly decorated, the gardens I spent so much time in planting my favorite flowers, kayaking and hiking, etc. Now because of an overwhelming loneliness I began to get mad. Oh shit, here was the anger again.

I struggled when my ex's birthday arrived, and I cried when our anniversary went by. I tried to convince myself that our relationship was never any good to begin with. Everything about it was bad, so why did I miss it? How could my spouse do this to me? I felt as if my partner never loved me and I began to believe that what I thought was a good relationship was really a bad one. My ex ruined everything and I wasted all my time being in that relationship.

Christmas was always my favorite time of year, but on the first Christmas as a divorced person, I felt sad and alone. I blamed my ex. I blamed myself for ever being involved with my ex, and then I got angry because here I was still letting my ex and the relationship, have control over me. I was letting it ruin my favorite holiday of the year.

It's at times like these that you will feel like you took one big step forward and now you're going two backwards. Will it ever end?

On Christmas day, I picked up my journal to write how sad I was but instead went back a few pages and read what I wrote about this phase of the breakup. I realized something very important. All of my thoughts had one thing in common; struggling when their birthday arrived, crying when our anniversary went by, missing my home, gardens, activities—**the void**s that were created by all of these things. I had blank spaces in my life and I needed to fill them, but not just go through the motions of filling them. I had to fill them with all the things that would make *me* happy.

Still, how could I do the things that my ex and I did

together? It would be too painful. I was angry at them for ruining all the things I enjoyed, for destroying any good feelings I had about our relationship. In a way, I was feeling sorry for myself.

You will cheat yourself as a person if you throw out all the good things you experienced during your relationship.

Your relationship wasn't worthless or a total waste of your time or you wouldn't have been there to begin with. There were a lot of good things (there had to be some even if it was just a few) and you shouldn't let go of them. You need to embrace them and once you let go of feeling sorry for yourself, you will see that.

So on that Christmas day, I made myself remember the good times I had during this holiday with my ex and even though those times were gone, I realized I needed to take the holiday I loved so much and enjoy it to the fullest. There would be new and better memories. Either way, I would not let the breakup take away my enjoyment of such a wonderful holiday.

When I wrote in my journal the next day, I set about finding all the things I liked to do before I met my ex as well as during the time I was with them. I also wrote down a few things I wanted to try—like zip lining, and places I wanted to go—like Hawaii (which I did with my sister and it was wonderful).

When the loneliness hits, you need to find those things that bring happiness to you and involve yourself in them. It is so vital to your mental and emotional health to find what other things have meaning to you that can replace what you've lost. Substitutions will soon become normal and won't be substitutions anymore—they will just become your happiness.

This is the time to find new things that excite you—to do the things you wanted to when you were with your spouse or partner but didn't for whatever reason, to go places you love to be (like Disneyworld!!) and find new places to explore (like Hawaii). Find the person you used to be and discover the person you can become. It is a new and exciting chapter in your life.

In your journal, write down all the things you loved

to do before you were with your spouse. Then write down the things you enjoyed doing when you and your spouse were together and know that you may have to modify them a little bit—like watching movies that you enjoy even though it might be by yourself, but now you can watch the "chick flick" that you couldn't when you were sitting with your spouse. Get a new puppy, but get one from the pound that needs a home instead of the purebred Rottweiler that your other half wanted.

Find new meaning in a lone hike in the woods. Enjoy the sound of the birds and the wind rustling the leaves on the trees instead of focusing on making sure your spouse is enjoying it. It's time for you to enjoy your life and to start worrying about you. If you find your substitutions, you will find your happiness and a happy you will be better able to take care of yourself and your children if you have any.

In finding your substitutions, you will be well on your way to self-discovery and making revelations that will help you to live a very full and happy life.

My Journal: What Are My Substitutions?

Name_____

Date_____

What things did you used to do before you were in a relationship?

_____

_____

_____

_____

_____

_____

_____

_____

_____

_____

_____

_____

_____

_____

_____

When you got into a relationship, what things did you stop doing?

_____

_____

_____

_____

_____

_____

_____

_____

_____

_____

_____

_____

_____

_____

_____

_____

_____

_____

What do you miss doing?

_____

_____

_____

_____

_____

_____

_____

_____

_____

_____

_____

_____

_____

_____

_____

_____

_____

What things would you like to do in the future?

_____

_____

_____

_____

What activities do you like to do that make you happy?

_____

_____

_____

_____

_____

_____

_____

_____

_____

_____

_____

_____

_____

_____

_____

_____

_____

_____

What are the places you like to go to, visit?

_____

_____

_____

_____

_____

_____

_____

_____

_____

_____

_____

_____

_____

_____

_____

_____

_____

_____

_____

_____

Where would you like to go that you've never been
before?

_____

_____

_____

_____

_____

Step 7: Self-Discovery and Revelation

Now is the step where you will self-evaluate. You're going to discover the things you might want to change about yourself and/or about the world around you, your expectations for a new job or a new relationship. It is a step of enlightenment in which you will become aware of who you are, who you want to be and what you want out of life.

The most important thing you can do for yourself is to find forgiveness, not only for your spouse but for yourself as well.

Forgiveness is one of the most difficult gifts to give to another, even harder sometimes to give it to yourself. It is also one of the most important and valuable things you can do to help you really feel free of the breakup, of your relationship and to find true happiness.

You might think that you worked through your anger so it will be easy to forgive, but it isn't always that way. If you can't forgive, then you still have some residual anger in there somewhere that stands in your way. You may never be able to get past it and that's okay. As I said, it's not easy to forgive.

But, if it is something that you want to do but don't feel you have it in you just yet, then go back and read the part of your journal on your emotions and your anger. You will need to do some more work here. Examine why you were angry in the beginning, then start a new journal page and try to write about it. Write down this question: Why can't I forgive my spouse? If you answer it truthfully, you will be able to decide if it's something you want to continue to work on, or if you just need to leave it alone.

You don't need to contact your spouse and tell them you forgive them, you just need to feel it and believe it in your heart.

If you still find you just aren't ready to forgive your

spouse or may never be able to, as I said, that's okay. It won't stop you from moving on in the process because you are now aware that this may be something you can't do and acknowledging this fact is enough to help you move forward. You just made your first self-discovery.

Now, one of the most important things you need to do is to forgive yourself. Why? Because somewhere in this process you found something you needed to forgive yourself for—whether it's the part you played in the breakdown of your relationship (maybe you let someone take away your power and control) or maybe there were things you said or did during the breakup that you regret. Be good and gentle to yourself. You deserve it. Forgive yourself so you can move on.

This is the time where you should be thinking "I finally got it." The light bulb has turned on. "I'm not as bad as I thought I was." This is the moment you realize that you really are beginning to figure this all out.

Now, you need to recognize happiness.

I was tired of writing about bad things that happened to me and the negative emotions those events caused. This thought brought me to the realization that I was ready for the next step—I wanted to read positive things about my life in my journal. I wanted to read about happy times and my accomplishments. I needed to read that I had changed myself and my life for the better and that I did learn important lessons. I wanted to see on the pages that I was proud of myself for getting through my breakup and coming out better on the other side. I was ready to really move on.

But as always, there is still some more work to do because the Energizer bunny isn't out of battery power just yet.

I already had some self-discoveries and revelations that had pushed to the forefront from all the previous writing I had done through my journaling, but it was only the beginning. Going back and reading, I slowly began to recognize that my relationship didn't fall apart solely because of my ex and it definitely didn't fall apart on its own. It was time to re-examine our life together and own up to the part I played in the ultimate betrayal. I didn't want to make the same mistakes twice so I first had to recognize the ones I made.

Believe it or not, this was the most difficult journaling process to begin. I couldn't write "I am pissed" because I wasn't anymore. I wasn't sad, I wasn't hurt. In fact, staring at the blank page made me realize the only sentence I could write that would begin this phase was "I am happy." Then I added one more. "I want to find love again and this time do it right."

If you really think about it, there is no way to know if you are doing it right. Everyone is different, so every relationship will be different. There were fundamental mistakes I made that I accepted and I knew I didn't want to repeat.

But let's face it, no one is perfect and life really is about making mistakes. There's nothing wrong with that. It's what you do with them that count. Do you truly learn from them? Or do you still repeat them over and over. Once again I am reminded of that phrase someone told me—"if you keep doing what you always did, then you will get what you always got." Makes sense to me because I kept going back to my ex and in turn, I kept getting dumped. I had to stop making the same mistake and figure out why I did it so I could stop doing it. That is what's called learning from your mistakes.

I also knew that the next person I fell in love with would have their faults just like I have mine and I wanted to be aware of it so we could learn to deal with them together in a way that strengthened the relationship, not break it down.

It was here I decided to make vows that I would abide by when I entered a new relationship—like really listening. Hearing and listening are two different things. I could hear everything my spouse said to me. Every word. But did all those words enter the section of my brain where they stayed so my mind would work through them to make sure if there were any actions I needed to take, I took them? Or did my partner's words enter one ear, pass through my brain and seep out the other one.

I also promised to stand up for myself more but to try and do it in a way that would help the other person to understand my quandary so it would encourage conversation and not fighting. Of course, I also realized that the other person might have the same struggles with the hearing and listening issues, but at least I would be aware of it and put forth the effort.

It was here that I became happy with myself once again. I didn't need to lose thirty pounds to attract someone. If I did, then it would never be a real relationship and I came to the revelation that mine had been based a lot on my looks.

When I got comfortable in my relationship, I started to dress down. I don't think that's wrong, but you have to know if your partner/spouse is expecting you to look dolled up all the time or if they are okay with a pair of sweats and a t-shirt. I decided that since I really didn't like to be "dolled" up *all* the time, I wouldn't dress up as much on future dates. I wanted the person to like me for me, not the way I dressed, or how long my hair was. (I wanted to cut my hair but my spouse was insistent that I didn't. They liked it long—guess what? Now it's short and I love it).

Where do you draw the line on these things?

More writing brought me to the only conclusion I

could make. Life had to work for me and that would only happen if I lived my life for who I really was. I had to be happy because if I wasn't, then my relationship wouldn't be a happy one. BAM!!! The light bulb went on again. I wasn't a piece of shit. I wasn't undesirable. I just wasn't true to myself. I understood I just didn't want to *be* what my ex wanted me to be. I tried. I couldn't.

When I had worked on my list of what was good about our marriage and what was bad, there was a long list of things that my spouse criticized me about, ways they expected me to be and things they expected me to do. I wouldn't say I was blind to it when I was with them. I would say I ignored the fact that I was trying really hard to please my spouse, not me and because of that I eventually started to buck the system, so to speak. So my partner went looking for someone else who they thought could be exactly what they wanted and wouldn't resist their control.

What a revelation to finally understand the crux of my relationship I had with my spouse and a big reason for its failure. I couldn't be mad or angry at myself, and I couldn't be mad at them anymore.

When we first met, I thought I wanted to be everything my ex desired in me and what they thought I was and should be, and maybe I did at the time, but remember what I said in the first chapter?

We change, so relationships will also change and if we can't grow and change with them, then there's not a real, deep and honest love that is and should be the true foundation for a relationship.

Taking the time to discover the real you will only enhance your life. Writing in your journal about your day's events, your feelings, your goals and hopes and dreams will be like solving a math problem or a crossword puzzle. You will feel elated when it all comes together and you find the answers. You will be happy. Really happy.

My Journal: My Self-Discovery and Revelations

Name_____

Date_____

What were the good things about my relationship?

_____

_____

_____

_____

_____

_____

_____

_____

_____

_____

_____

_____

_____

_____

_____

_____

What were the bad things about my relationship?

_____

_____

_____

_____

_____

_____

_____

_____

_____

_____

What did they do wrong?

_____

_____

_____

_____

_____

_____

_____

_____

_____

_____

_____

_____

_____

_____

What did I do wrong? What were my mistakes?

_____

_____

_____

_____

What did I learn from my mistakes—what not to repeat?

_____

_____

_____

_____

_____

_____

_____

_____

_____

_____

_____

_____

_____

_____

_____

_____

_____

_____

What could I have done better?

_____

_____

_____

_____

_____

_____

_____

_____

_____

_____

_____

_____

_____

_____

_____

_____

_____

_____

_____

What do I expect in a relationship and in love?

_____

_____

_____

How do I want to be treated?

_____

_____

_____

_____

_____

_____

_____

_____

_____

_____

_____

_____

_____

_____

_____

_____

_____

_____

_____

_____

What do I expect from my life?

_____

_____

_____

_____

_____

_____

_____

_____

_____

_____

_____

_____

_____

_____

_____

_____

_____

_____

_____

What are the substitutions I found that make me happy?

_____

_____

_____

_____

Step 8: Owning Your Life Through Owning Your Journal

Be Proud. Be Strong. Be Happy.

And keep journaling. That is what step 8 is for—to help you to continue to stay on your path to happiness, to continue to be strong and proud of all you do.

Of course, journaling is not foolproof and it doesn't necessarily solve everything, but it will help. You will make mistakes—like I did when I went back. You will learn from your mistakes and at the end when it is really finally over, you need to make sure you own those mistakes. This is a very valuable outcome from journaling.

Once again I will be honest with you. When I reached this point, I stopped journaling—not totally though—I just didn't think I needed it as much as I did through the whole process of my breakup. But when I picked up a pen and paper to write this book, I have to admit it was like writing another journal. The process was cathartic and enlightening and I realized that maybe the process is never really over.

In a sense, writing this book helped me to own my previous journals. I actually have three notebooks worth of writing from my breakup. I still hold on to them but I haven't read them since I reached this point. The first two journals are full of painful memories that I don't want to revisit. They're done, in the past and that is where I want to keep them, but I own those journals. I own that story and I own the process I went through to reach where I am today. By owning my journals that were filled with my stories, my emotions, my mistakes and my discoveries, I was able to take back my life.

Now you need to own your life, which only you can do. No one else can unless we give them the control and you don't want to do that anymore. So start by facing your fears. You might be afraid of someone else coming into your life and taking control again because you gave it up once before. But you made it this far. Tell yourself you won't let that happen.

There are some things you can do to prevent yourself from ever letting it happen again.

First, start making the changes you promised yourself throughout your journaling. Start doing the things you've always wanted to do. I did. I went zip lining and it was the most exhilarating fun I've ever had. I screamed in joy the whole way down!
You also need to continue to make goals and lists of thing you want to do and places you want to go. And then do them. It's also really good to dream…and dream big. You can accomplish anything you put your mind to. I did. I wrote this book and I am proud of my accomplishment and the possibility of helping other people to achieve what they feel they might not be able to.

All of this will help you to build your self-esteem back up. You can't say it hasn't been knocked down. Let's face it, when your spouse leaves you for someone else, no matter how hard you try, it can knock your self-esteem down at least a little, sometimes a lot.

Take a look in the mirror and see what a beautiful person you are. Give yourself permission to be who you want to be and live the life you want to live. It might be a little overwhelming at this point because you're still not sure what that is but you actually already started that journey when you journaled about your substitutions and self-discovery. So see, you've got a good start. Go back to those two sections of your journal and read and re-read and start living it because true ownership is the life you make for yourself, not the one that is mapped out for you by someone else.

There are also two things you always need to remember and they are important for you to stay on your chosen path. The first is now that you are taking control of your life, living it the way you want to, you must always think about the consequences of your actions and take responsibility for them—good or bad. If you own your life, then you must own you're your mistakes and the consequences.

The second thing is to own your accomplishments.

Don't hide them in the shadows. Recognize them, be proud of them, and stand tall because this whole journey is about what you accomplished and what you can accomplish, not what you can't.

Journaling isn't for everyone and it's not always easy. Some people just don't like to write. But it doesn't hurt to give it a try. What have you got to lose? Well, your anger, fear, and sadness for one thing. Journaling will help you to lasso those emotions and take control of them. It might just help you to push through the breakup and stand up for yourself, for your happiness. But remember, it does not happen overnight.

Healing, of any kind, takes time and it takes a different amount of time for everyone. Be patient and gentle with yourself. If you find that it's taking you too long to progress forward because you can't seem to get a hold of and move past your negative emotions, then it might be time to get help.

Journaling through your breakup can keep you sane and in control and I hope what you see after this journey is a better, happier you. I also hope journaling kept you from gaining too much weight

131

(if it did, you can still enjoy that Cookie Dough ice cream now and then) or getting too thin (if you did, then you need to enjoy that Cookie Dough ice cream a little more than now and then).

My Journal: I Own My Life

Name_____

Date_____

What things are you going to change?

_____

_____

_____

_____

_____

_____

_____

_____

_____

_____

_____

_____

_____

_____

_____

_____

What makes you feel good about yourself?

_____

_____

_____

_____

_____

_____

_____

_____

_____

_____

_____

_____

_____

_____

_____

_____

_____

_____

What are your goals and how are you going to
achieve them?

_____

_____

_____

_____

_____

_____

_____

_____

_____

_____

_____

_____

_____

_____

_____

_____

_____

_____

_____

_____

What are your dreams and how are you going to achieve them?

_____

_____

_____

What made you happy today?

_____

_____

_____

_____

_____

_____

_____

_____

_____

_____

_____

_____

_____

_____

_____

_____

_____

_____

_____

Did I stray from my path today? If so why and what can I do to get back on track?

_____

_____

_____

_____

_____

_____

_____

_____

What were your accomplishments today?

You Made It!

I hope you're reading this chapter because you completed you're journey to a better, stronger and happier you. But don't let the journey end here. Continue your journaling, not only on the bad days but on the good days as well because now, there will be more of those.

If you run into a problem at work or with a friend, write it in your journal to help you search for the answers. And when you start dating again, write about your dates and all the good feelings you are experiencing.

You can use this journal process to help you through any adverse events that might happen in your life whether it be the loss of a job, or the loss of a loved one. Just replace the word "breakup" in the title with whatever occurrence you are experiencing (ex-Journaling Through the Loss of My Job). Let the journal process continue to help better your life.

I have. In fact, writing this book for you was my

latest journal. I wanted more out of my breakup and when I wrote that down one day, the thought of helping others was first and foremost what I wanted from it. If I can ease the pain for you just a little and make you believe that there is light at the end of the tunnel, then we have all succeeded – I believe you can succeed.

So I would love to hear about your journey. Feel free to contact me at nancenewman.com. Share with me your success story. And if you liked my book, it would be great if you would do me the honor of leaving a review on Amazon.com.

There are extra journaling pages at the end of this book. You can also download a free file that contains journal pages from this book for you to use during your own process. Just go to nancenewman.com. Go to the Bookshelf tab and then click on this book.

Thanks for sharing in my journey.

About the Author

After going through a very difficult and heartbreaking divorce by journaling my way through it, I wanted to help others to find their way. I hope journaling does for you what it did for me— it helped me to heal and to move on to live a happy, healthy, and fulfilling life.

I've been writing ever since I can remember-- journals, songs, fiction novels and now my first non-fiction book. In between work and writing, I take care of my two senior dogs, a boxer and a rescued Min Pin. I enjoy being active in the outdoors in all four seasons partaking in many different activities. I also play guitar, write music and sing in a duo having produced our first album of love songs in 2015.

I firmly believe it's never too late to make your dreams a reality. Becoming an author has been my dream and after twenty years working in Motion Picture film at a once top company, a short stint as a physical education teacher, and ten more years as a head bus driver for a school district where I get to solve the puzzle of setting up bus routes for thousands of students, it's time.

Still…sometimes, you might see me driving a big yellow school bus.

Please visit www.nancenewman.com to find out more about my books and music!

Journaling Through a Breakup

How to Effectively Cope Through a Breakup Without Gaining 50 lbs. or Becoming Anorexic

Extra Journaling Pages

My Journal
My Breakup

Name_____

Date_____

How did your breakup happen?

_____

_____

_____

_____

_____

_____

_____

_____

_____

_____

_____

_____

_____

_____

_____

How did you feel when they told you?

_____

_____

_____

_____

_____

_____

_____

_____

_____

_____

_____

_____

_____

_____

_____

_____

_____

_____

_____

What things will you need to work through after the breakup (move, divide possessions, pets, friends, children, and family)?

_____

_____

_____

_____

_____

_____

_____

_____

_____

_____

_____

_____

_____

_____

_____

_____

_____

_____

_____

How does it make you feel?

_____

_____

_____

My Journal
My Breakup

Name_____
Date_____

How did your breakup happen?

_____

_____

_____

_____

_____

_____

_____

_____

_____

_____

_____

_____

_____

_____

_____

How did you feel when they told you?

_____

_____

_____

_____

_____

_____

_____

_____

_____

_____

_____

_____

_____

_____

_____

_____

_____

_____

_____

What things will you need to work through after the breakup (move, divide possessions, pets, friends, children, and family)?

_____

_____

_____

How does it make you feel?

_____

_____

_____

_____

_____

_____

_____

_____

_____

_____

_____

_____

_____

_____

_____

_____

_____

_____

_____

My Journal
My Breakup

Name_____
Date_____

How did your breakup happen?

_____

_____

_____

_____

_____

_____

_____

_____

_____

_____

_____

_____

_____

_____

_____

How did you feel when they told you?

_____

_____

_____

_____

_____

_____

_____

_____

_____

_____

_____

_____

_____

_____

_____

_____

_____

_____

_____

_____

What things will you need to work through after the breakup (move, divide possessions, pets, friends, children, and family)?

_____

_____

_____

How does it make you feel?

_____

_____

_____

_____

_____

_____

_____

_____

_____

_____

_____

_____

_____

_____

_____

_____

_____

_____

My Journal
My Breakup

Name_____

Date_____

How did your breakup happen?

_____

_____

_____

_____

_____

_____

_____

_____

_____

_____

_____

_____

_____

_____

How did you feel when they told you?

_____

_____

_____

What things will you need to work through after the breakup (move, divide possessions, pets, friends, children, and family)?

_____

_____

_____

_____

_____

_____

_____

_____

_____

_____

_____

_____

_____

_____

_____

_____

_____

_____

_____

_____

How does it make you feel?

_____

_____

_____

_____

_____

_____

_____

_____

_____

_____

_____

_____

_____

_____

_____

_____

_____

_____

_____

My Journal
My Breakup

Name_____

Date_____

How did your breakup happen?

_____

_____

_____

_____

_____

_____

_____

_____

_____

_____

_____

_____

_____

_____

_____

_____

How did you feel when they told you?

_____

_____

_____

What things will you need to work through after the
breakup (move, divide possessions, pets, friends,
children, and family)?

_____

_____

_____

_____

_____

_____

_____

_____

_____

_____

_____

_____

_____

_____

_____

_____

_____

_____

How does it make you feel?

_____

_____

_____

_____

_____

_____

_____

_____

_____

_____

_____

_____

_____

_____

_____

_____

_____

_____

_____

_____

_____

_____

_____

My Journal
My Breakup

Name_____

Date_____

How did your breakup happen?

_____

_____

_____

_____

_____

_____

_____

_____

_____

_____

_____

_____

How did you feel when they told you?

_____

_____

_____

_____

_____

_____

What things will you need to work through after the
breakup (move, divide possessions, pets, friends,
children, and family)?

_____

_____

_____

_____

_____

_____

_____

_____

_____

_____

_____

_____

_____

_____

_____

_____

_____

_____

How does it make you feel?

_____

_____

_____

_____

My Journal
My Breakup

Name_____
Date_____

How did your breakup happen?

_____

_____

_____

_____

_____

_____

_____

_____

_____

_____

_____

_____

_____

_____

_____

How did you feel when they told you?

_____

_____

_____

_____

_____

_____

_____

_____

_____

_____

_____

_____

_____

_____

_____

_____

_____

_____

_____

What things will you need to work through after the breakup (move, divide possessions, pets, friends, children, and family)?

_____

_____

_____

_____

_____

_____

_____

_____

_____

_____

_____

_____

_____

_____

_____

_____

_____

_____

_____

_____

_____

How does it make you feel?

_____

_____

_____

My Journal
My Breakup

Name_____

Date_____

How did your breakup happen?

_____

_____

_____

_____

_____

_____

_____

_____

_____

_____

_____

_____

_____

_____

_____

How did you feel when they told you?

_____

_____

_____

_____

_____

_____

_____

_____

_____

_____

_____

_____

_____

_____

_____

_____

_____

_____

_____

What things will you need to work through after the breakup (move, divide possessions, pets, friends, children, and family)?

_____

_____

How does it make you feel?

_____

_____

_____

_____

_____

My Journal
My Breakup

Name_____

Date_____

How did your breakup happen?

_____

_____

_____

_____

_____

_____

_____

_____

_____

_____

_____

_____

_____

_____

How did you feel when they told you?

_____

_____

_____

_____

_____

_____

_____

_____

_____

_____

_____

_____

_____

_____

_____

_____

_____

_____

_____

_____

What things will you need to work through after the
breakup (move, divide possessions, pets, friends,

children, and family)?

_____

_____

_____

_____

_____

_____

_____

_____

_____

_____

_____

_____

_____

_____

_____

_____

_____

_____

How does it make you feel?

_____

_____

_____

_____

_____

_____

_____

_____

_____

_____

_____

_____

_____

_____

_____

_____

_____

_____

_____

My Journal
Explore My Emotions

Name_____

Date_____

Do you feel sad? Why?

_____

_____

_____

_____

_____

_____

_____

_____

_____

_____

_____

_____

_____

_____

_____

_____

_____

Do you feel angry? Why?

_____

_____

Do you feel inadequate? Why?

_____

_____

_____

_____

_____

_____

Are you afraid? Why?

_____

_____

_____

_____

_____

_____

_____

_____

_____

_____

_____

_____

_____

_____

_____

_____

_____

_____

_____

Are you sleeping at night? If not, what is keeping you up?

_____

_____

_____

_____

_____

_____

_____

_____

_____

_____

_____

_____

_____

_____

_____

_____

_____

_____

_____

_____

Do you find yourself not wanting to do anything but sleep or lay on the couch all day?

_____

_____

_____

Are you binging on food or are you not eating?
What are you eating?

_____

_____

_____

_____

_____

_____

_____

_____

_____

_____

_____

How often are you crying? What makes you cry?

_____

_____

_____

_____

_____

_____

_____

_____

_____

_____

_____

_____

Are you accepting what's happened? If not, why aren't you?

_____

_____

Are you feeling regrets? Why?

_____

_____

_____

_____

_____

_____

Are you confused, unsure of what to do next? Why?

_____

_____

_____

_____

_____

_____

_____

_____

_____

_____

_____

_____

_____

_____

_____

_____

_____

_____

_____

_____

_____

_____

Do you feel like a failure? Why do you think you're a failure?

_____

_____

_____

_____

_____

_____

_____

_____

_____

_____

_____

_____

_____

_____

_____

_____

_____

_____

_____

_____

_____

Do you want revenge? What do you think getting revenge will do for you?

Is it worth the consequences?

_____

_____

_____

_____

_____

_____

_____

_____

_____

_____

_____

_____

_____

_____

_____

_____

_____

_____

My Journal
Have Some Fun-Fantasize

Name_____
Date_____

Draw a picture here of what you would like to do to your spouse.

Write down here all the things you would like to do. Make them as outrageous and fun as you can—not realistic.

_____

_____

_____

_____

_____

_____

_____

_____

_____

_____

_____

_____

_____

_____

_____

_____

_____

_____

_____

_____

Draw pictures of some of those things you listed above.

My Journal
My Kiss Off Letter

Name_____

Date_____

Dear…………,

I am done with you.

_____

_____

_____

_____

_____

_____

_____

_____

_____

_____

_____

_____

_____

_____

_____

_____

_____

_____

_____

My Journal
What Are My Substitutions?

Name_____

Date_____

What things did you used to do before you were in a relationship?

_____

_____

_____

_____

_____

_____

_____

_____

_____

_____

_____

_____

_____

_____

When you got into a relationship, what things did you stop doing?

What do you miss doing?

_____

_____

_____

_____

_____

_____

_____

_____

What things would you like to do in the future?

_____

_____

_____

_____

_____

_____

_____

_____

_____

_____

_____

_____

_____

_____

_____

_____

_____

_____

_____

_____

What activities do you like to do that make you happy?

_____

_____

What are the places you like to go to, visit?

_____

_____

_____

_____

_____

_____

Where would you like to go that you've never been
before?

_____

_____

_____

_____

_____

_____

_____

_____

_____

_____

_____

_____

_____

_____

_____

_____

_____

_____

_____

_____

My Journal
My Self-Discovery and Revelations

Name_____
Date_____

What were the good things about my relationship?

_____

_____

_____

_____

_____

_____

_____

_____

_____

_____

_____

_____

_____

_____

_____

_____

_____

What were the bad things about my relationship?

_____

_____

_____

_____

What did my spouse, partner do wrong?

_____

_____

_____

_____

_____

_____

_____

_____

_____

_____

_____

_____

What did I do wrong? What were my mistakes?

What did I learn from my mistakes—what not to repeat?

What could I have done better?

_____

_____

_____

_____

_____

_____

What do I expect in a relationship and in love?

_____

_____

_____

_____

_____

_____

_____

_____

_____

_____

_____

_____

_____

_____

_____

_____

_____

_____

_____

_____

_____

How do I want to be treated?

_____

_____

_____

_____

What do I expect from my life?

_____

_____

_____

_____

_____

_____

_____

_____

_____

_____

_____

_____

_____

What are the substitutions I found that make me happy?

_____

_____

_____

_____

_____

_____

_____

_____

_____

_____

My Journal
I Own My Life

Name_____
Date_____

What things am I going to change?

_____

_____

_____

_____

_____

_____

_____

_____

_____

_____

_____

_____

_____

What makes me feel good about myself?

_____

_____

_____

_____

What are my goals and how am I going to achieve them?

_____

_____

_____

_____

_____

_____

_____

_____

_____

_____

_____

_____

_____

_____

_____

_____

_____

What are my dreams and how am I going to achieve them?

_____

_____

_____

_____

_____

_____

_____

_____

_____

_____

_____

_____

_____

_____

_____

_____

_____

_____

What made me happy today?

_____

_____

_____

Did I stray from my path today? If so why and what can I do to get back on track?

_____

_____

_____

_____

_____

_____

What were my accomplishments today?

_____

_____

_____

_____

_____

_____

_____

_____

_____

_____

_____

_____

_____

_____

_____

_____

_____

_____

_____

_____

My Journal
I Own My Life

Name_____

Date_____

What are my goals for today and how am I going to

achieve them?

_____

_____

_____

_____

_____

_____

_____

_____

_____

_____

_____

_____

_____

What made me happy today?

_____

_____

_____

_____

Did I stray from my path today? If so why and what can I do to get back on track?

_____

_____

_____

_____

_____

_____

_____

_____

_____

_____

_____

_____

_____

_____

_____

_____

_____

_____

What were my accomplishments today?

_____

_____

_____

_____

_____

_____

_____

_____

_____

_____

_____

_____

_____

_____

_____

_____

_____

_____

_____

My Journal
I Own My Life

Name_____

Date_____

What are my goals for today and how am I going to
achieve them?

_____

_____

_____

_____

_____

_____

_____

_____

_____

_____

_____

_____

_____

What made me happy today?

_____

_____

_____

_____

_____

_____

_____

Did I stray from my path today? If so why and what can I do to get back on track?

_____

_____

_____

_____

_____

_____

_____

_____

_____

_____

_____

_____

_____

_____

_____

_____

_____

_____

_____

What were my accomplishments today?

_____

_____

_____

_____

My Journal
I Own My Life

Name_____

Date_____

What are my goals for today and how am I going to achieve them?

_____

_____

_____

_____

_____

_____

_____

_____

_____

_____

What made me happy today?

Did I stray from my path today? If so why and what can I do to get back on track?

_____

_____

_____

_____

_____

_____

_____

_____

_____

_____

_____

_____

_____

What were my accomplishments today?

_____

_____

_____

_____

My Journal
I Own My Life

Name_____

Date_____

What are my goals for today and how am I going to achieve them?

_____

_____

_____

_____

_____

_____

_____

What made me happy today?

_____

_____

_____

_____

_____

_____

_____

_____

_____

_____

_____

Did I stray from my path today? If so why and what can I do to get back on track?

_____

_____

What were my accomplishments today?

_____

_____

_____

_____

_____

_____

My Journal
I Own My Life

Name_____

Date_____

What are my goals for today and how am I going to achieve them?

_____

_____

_____

_____

_____

_____

_____

_____

_____

_____

_____

_____

_____

What made me happy today?

_____

_____

_____

_____

_____

_____

_____

_____

_____

_____

_____

_____

_____

_____

_____

_____

_____

_____

_____

_____

_____

Did I stray from my path today? If so why and what can I do to get back on track?

What were my accomplishments today?

_____

_____

_____

_____

_____

_____

_____

_____

My Journal
I Own My Life

Name_____

Date_____

What are my goals for today and how am I going to achieve them?

_____

_____

_____

_____

_____

_____

_____

_____

_____

_____

_____

_____

_____

What made me happy today?

_____

_____

_____

Did I stray from my path today? If so why and what can I do to get back on track?

_____

_____

_____

_____

_____

_____

_____

_____

_____

_____

_____

_____

_____

_____

_____

_____

_____

_____

_____

What were my accomplishments today?

_____

_____

_____

_____

_____

_____

_____

_____

_____

_____

_____

_____

_____

_____

_____

_____

_____

_____

_____

_____

_____

My Journal
I Own My Life

Name_____

Date_____

What are my goals for today and how am I going to

achieve them?

_____

_____

_____

_____

_____

_____

_____

_____

_____

_____

_____

_____

What made me happy today?

Did I stray from my path today? If so why and what can I do to get back on track?

_____

_____

_____

_____

_____

_____

_____

_____

What were my accomplishments today?

_____

_____

_____

_____

_____

_____

_____

_____

_____

_____

_____

_____

_____

_____

_____

_____

_____

_____

My Journal
I Own My Life

Name_____

Date_____

What are my goals for today and how am I going to achieve them?

_____

_____

_____

_____

_____

_____

_____

_____

_____

_____

_____

_____

_____

What made me happy today?

_____

_____

_____

_____

_____

_____

Did I stray from my path today? If so why and what can I do to get back on track?

_____

_____

_____

_____

_____

_____

_____

_____

_____

_____

_____

_____

_____

_____

_____

_____

_____

_____

What were my accomplishments today?

_____

_____

_____

_____

Made in the USA
Middletown, DE
27 October 2022

13641992R00168